Gather the Pieces

Breaking Free from a Broken Heart

© Copyright 2018 by Kylelashay Draper

All rights reserved. No part of this book may be reproduced, scanned, or distributed in any printed or electronic form without permission. Please do not participate in or encourage piracy of copyrighted materials in violation of the author's rights. Purchase only authorized editions.

ISBN-13: 978-1986497848
ISBN-10: 1986497844

*To Denisha Karim and
Latoya Golden*

*You have always been my
strength when the world didn't
know I was falling apart.
Bad boys for life*

*Keep thy heart with all diligence, for out of it
are the issues of life.
(Proverbs 4:23 KJV)*

Table of Contents

The Breaking
The Man the Mirror and the Mirage

The First Few Days without You
Day 1
Day 2
Day 3

Trying to forget you
Day 7
Day 8
Day 9
Day 10
Day 11

Trying to face the facts
Day 12
Day 13
Day 14

Trying to Hate You
Day 16
Day 17

Trying to Keep You
Day 21
Day 25

You Pushed Me
Losing Balance
Slipping
Falling
Hanging on for Dear Life
Preparing for Landing
Shattering All Over the Ground

Trying to Numb the Pain
Sleeping Soundly
Woe'Man Down
Morphine for the Heart

Home Invasion
Stranger in my House
The Shelter of my Heart

Trying to Have a Heart for Revenge
But it won't Heal Me
Bittersweet

Beginning to Heal
Moving Forward
It's Working for Me

Learning to Love Myself Instead
The Day I Met You
Now What Do You See
I am Her, She is Me

This is Forgiveness
For Me, Not For You
Thank You!

Accepting Validation from God
My Temple
Be Still and Know
Things to Remember
On Repeat

The Breaking

The Man the Mirror and the Mirage

I met a man, a perfect man.
He was everything I thought I could ever need.
Charming, strong, intelligent, sweet; he was the perfect recipe.
He dotted all of his I's and crossed all of his T's.
This man would stay forever and he would never leave.
Gentle, kind and respectful, He was considerate in all of his doings.
He was dedicated to his goals; he knew the direction he was going.
His kisses were ever so passionate his voice always calm and collected.
He was a man who showed up spotless a man that made me feel protected.
But he told me about a mirage, this fantasy, this optical illusion.
I ignored the details that he gave to me and I drew my own conclusion.
He told me this mirage would seem so real that it could fool him and even fool me
This mirage was only a trick that came straight from the enemy.
Little did I know he was referring to he and I when he spoke of this mirage.
I was falling in love with an illusion, a cover up and a well kept facade.
This mirage felt so safe and secure even though in reality it didn't exist.

He told me that discovering this mirage would confuse me just like this.
Now I am left with a story to tell of a love that I fell in that was not real.
Where a man came in my life and made me fall in love with him.
And then told me that who I thought he was; was never really him.

Gather the Pieces

The First Few Days without You

Day 1:

I woke up happy

Feeling powerful

Like I had conquered a fear

I got dressed; did my hair

Looked myself in the mirror

Said my prayers

Took off for work and managed to arrive on time

I read a good book

Had a productive day

And for the gym I even made time

I had dinner

I showered

I sat in the closet with my own thoughts

I spoke to my sisters

Spoke to an old friend & we had an interesting talk

I lay in bed staring at the ceiling

Thought real hard about many things

I began to cry tears rolling to the sides of my eyes

I was acknowledging my feelings

I prayed again for peace and strength

Pulled my blankets back to prepare for sleep

I crawled into bed feeling a little bit better

I then wrote this piece

Day 2:

I woke up

I feel okay

I tell the lord thank you

I get ready for the day

I'm running a little behind

But I listen to an inspiring song

I stop to get coffee, hoping that it's strong

I walk into work with a smile

Despite the fact that I was late

I get setup at my desk with the hope of a marvelous day

I make some money, I help some people

I talk and laugh with the ones that sit near

I read a book written by Oprah

It tells me some things that I really need to hear

I smile to myself and I take deep breaths

I appreciate the now that I am in

I think about you a lot, ready and waiting for my shift to end

Before I leave I hug a friend

I say bye to the people on my team

I stop at the mall to get some things for myself

I come home; grab a blanket, and Häagen-Dazs ice cream
I take a call or actually a couple
I share a few words and a few laughs
I lie in bed and I think to myself
Do I like the place in life that I am at?
I answer yes then I make myself a promise
I will love and not become attached
I will live my life in happiness
I will not be focused on the future or past
I will be content with where I am
I will not jump the gun or rush
I will embrace today for what it is because it offers me so much

Day 3:

I didn't sleep much last night

Maybe 30 minutes to be exact

I stayed the night at a friend's house

We stayed up all night to get ready and pack

We headed to the airport around 4am

We were going to Miami, FL to celebrate

My best friend is turning 26; we're going for her birthday.

The trip there was smooth for the most part

I spent most of it asleep

I was exhausted from the night before

It finally caught up to me

We made it to our destination

I was Happy to have arrived

I realize how God has answered my prayers

I feel so much joy inside

I am surrounded by people who love and support me

And we're all doing what we love

To me, that's the biggest blessing that God has given us

I didn't think much about you today

I was too focused on those who are in my life

I'm proud to say I am where I am and I think I'm doing it right
I don't feel a sense of loss anymore
I feel like everything is working out
I trust the process God has for me
I don't have a shadow of doubt
I laugh and talk with my friends
We dance. We eat. we sing
In all these moments I come to understand what being "in love" really means

*And sometimes God sends people to rob you of your entire identity that you may then walk into your truest self.
What they take; let them have.*

Trying to Forget You

Day 7:

Today I woke up at 5:45 am
I rolled out of bed and turned off my alarm
I turned on the lights
I stretched and thanked God
I began getting dressed for the morning
I made my bed and left the house
I was running on a good time
I prayed a bit and listened to some gospel
I wanted to free my mind
I had time for coffee and breakfast
I stopped to grab it then headed to work
I knew today would be a great day
I planned for productivity
I finished my first book
I thought about you today
I began to become a little sad
I started writing this to distract myself
I am choosing not to feel like that
I believe that I will succeed
I believe that everything will be fine
I believe that everything that I desire in life is already mine

Day 8:

Today is the day I finally let go

No more you

No more us

No more of the idea of we

I called you and I think you were obedient

I think you did what I asked of you

I told you not to answer if I called

I told you not to respond if I texted

Because I knew I would eventually come back;

Back to the same hurt;

Back to the same "no this won't work."

Back to the hope that had no future in it.

So you cared for me by letting me go

Now I have to care for myself by letting you.

I feel deep down that still, maybe it isn't over

Maybe you really just need time

But then at the back of my mind I hear...

"This was only temporary."

A temporary pleasure

A temporary friendship

A temporary lesson

That should last me a lifetime.

I now have to figure out how I allowed myself to believe & then go and tell the whole world that someday, you would be my husband. And now that you're gone, I have to tell those same people whom I bragged to about how amazing you are that you are now no more. That you are now just a part of a memory, now just a part of a fantasy, now just a part of what used to be. You. I. us is only something I was imagining.

Day 9:

I really miss you

I keep thinking of you

I wish we could talk

I know I cut contact for a reason

I wish I didn't have to walk

I don't know if it was the right choice

I guess I'll see later on down the line

I am happy

I just wish my happiness would come from you still being a part of my life

I know that everything is working

And our separation is for the best on both ends

And if I wasn't in love with you I would still agree to us being friends

Maybe later on down the line I'll see the value in what we did I hope we each discover the true beauty in this

Day 10:

I get these random urges of sadness when I think of not having you.

I hate that we so quickly ended; at times it doesn't seem real or true.

I accept never having you again; I'll be okay if you never return.

I'll accept you as a lesson and from it I will learn.

I will be happy in my own life and live freely despite how it hurts sometimes.

You taught me not to get attached to anything or anyone that isn't mine.

I do hope we actually work but if we don't, I still will love again.

I hope you will love again too, you deserve a second chance.

I hope all is well with you, I hope you're happy in life.

I hope that everything you pursue turns out to be right.

I won't be broken because I lost you; you brought me so many smiles while you were here.

I know I will find someone else as great as you, I choose not to walk in fear.

Day 11:

I am happy

It's true...

but I still miss you

I have all that I want and need but I still desire you

I am walking in my purpose

I know I am on the right path

I know that in due time if you are mine you will come back

My heart is heavy on certain days

When I think that truly and forever we are done

I hope that if that is the case I can forget what we had become

I believe that everything happens for a reason

I haven't yet discovered that in what happened with you and I

But I pray every day I can find clarity in what's inside

I still do everything the same

I just do it without you

I can't believe how accustomed I had gotten to being in routine with you

Talking to you all the time has turned into browsing the web

And when I wake up I talk to God instead of sending you a good morning text
I know in time I will let go but for now I will write until this feeling fades
I will write until I forget my own desires and let us continue on in our own way

Don't let defeat become your final chapter,
Keep writing until you find your happy ending.

Trying to Face the Facts

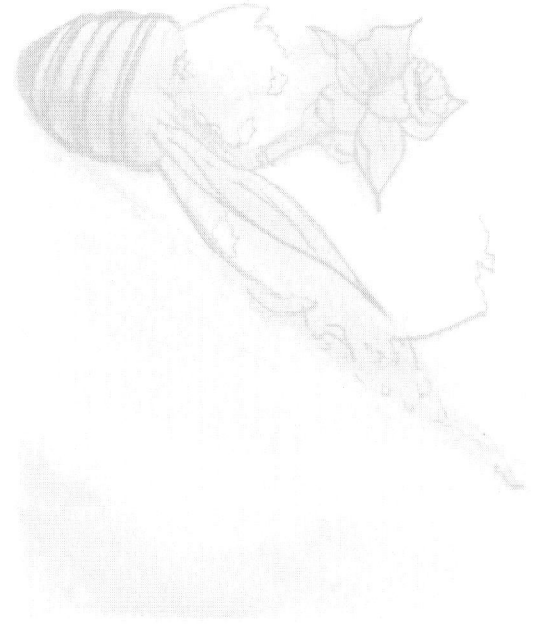

Day 12:

What if I was really wrong?

What if you're really not the one?

What if everything I saw in you was only an illusion derived from my need to be loved?

What if I had all the signs wrong & I only saw what I wanted to see?

What if it's true in fact that you never planned to be with me?

What if I never find another person who gets me like you do?

What if you never come back to me then what do I do?

What if I can't get over you and I can't bring myself to love again?

What if I never find another man that can love me like you can?

What if God calls you back to me would you ignore him or would you come?

What if you're fighting our destiny and for you I really am the one?

What if you're afraid to fall for me because you know what it's like to love and lose?

What if you didn't have to worry about that because I would never leave you?
What if this was all a mirage and everything we were was actually fake?
What if I was dreaming the entire time
& I thought I was awake?

Day 13:

I'm dreading the fact that I haven't spoken to you and the fact that I have blocked you on social media.
I think of you every single day wishing I could call and talk to you, that you would call me and say hello or maybe even that you've changed your mind.
Parts of me hang on to hope, parts of me say move forward and let go and I have let go but it still hurts because I miss how we laughed together.
How we talked endlessly about any and everything.
I have yet to laugh until my stomach hurts with anyone else.
I hope to discover someone who I can connect with as much as I connected with you.
I write this with the intention to remove the desire to email or text you and pour out all my weaknesses and vulnerabilities concerning you.
I am attempting to walk in dignity having lost someone I gave my all to.
I am happy despite my thoughts of you & I hope that you are happy too.

Day 14:

I reached out to you
I wanted to say hello
I still thought that you had me blocked
I wanted to for sure know
When I called you the phone rang
I was as nervous as I could be
I was hoping I had the wrong phone number
I was hoping you would ignore me
I know that sounds stupid
I genuinely wanted to hear you speak
I miss you like crazy everyday
I haven't spoken to you in 2 weeks
The phone rang but you did not answer
I was actually relieved
I had no idea what I would say to you
I didn't want you to think I was weak
But you called me back minutes later
Then you sent a text asking if I was okay
You said you were in class and asked if I needed anything
It made me happy that you were still attentive when it comes to me
We shared a couple of texts back and forth

You made me laugh as you always do
I cut the conversation short
I just needed to hear from you
I will now continue with my life
I may check in with you some other day
I understand that right now we can't be
I just wanted to know you were okay

Express how you feel without allowing ego to silence you; it's one of the highest forms of humility.

Trying to Hate You

Day 16:

I think I'm eating my sorrows away

All I want is food

I am not hungry even a little but eating is all I want to do

I can't keep you off my mind

I hate it with a passion

I want to forget that I ever knew you

I can't seem to shake the sadness

I hate that I know you exist

I hate that you ever made me smile
I hate that I loved your personality
I hate that I loved your style
I hate that you were so charming
I hate that you were always kind
Maybe those are all the reasons I can't seem to get you out of my mind

I know that this feeling will pass

I pray that it will as soon as can be

I know that time heals all things

I just hope "all" includes "me"

I am not saying I am broken without you

I am saying you brought me a joy I've never received from a man

I do pray that there is another out there that can make me as happy as you can

Day 17:

I have to forgive you daily
I have to tell myself to move on
I don't know why this is so hard; the process is taking so long
At times I still get angry
At times I still do cry
At times it's next to impossible to keep you off my mind
I try not to replay the events
I try not to ask what I did wrong
I try not to hurt myself by continuing to hold on
I have to tell myself that everything is okay
Even though at times nothing really is
I have to tell myself it is normal to feel pain when you go through something like this
I really don't want to be bitter
I really don't to be angry with you
That is why despite everything I continue to be kind to you
At times I don't want to be
At times I want to throw fits of rage
I want to hurt you like you hurt me
but I love you too much to cause you pain

I am gathering all of my pieces
I am praying for you, everyday
I am doing my best to hold fast to the good moments
& wish you well in every way

A liar can make you feel loved without ever loving you at all but never punish yourself for truly loving someone that didn't truly love you.

Trying to Keep You

Day 21:

It has been 21 days since I let you go
You showed up to my play on the 19th day it made me happier than you'll ever know.
I got to hug you so tight I didn't want to release you
I missed the way it felt to just hold you
Your scent was still the same, it clung to my clothes
And when you said you had to leave I didn't want you to go
But I understood the reasons and they're too deep to just ignore
but my heart was content that I got to hug you once more
Now its day 21 and it's like I'm starting back at day one
I love the fact that I saw your face and heard your voice but it ended too soon.
I am right back where I began with a longing for you to be mine
I really hate the fact that we had to cross paths at the wrong time
I am thinking of you a lot today hoping that I can keep you and I in Gods' hands

If you are mine and I am yours God will make a way for us to stand

If it is not so I just hope that I can continue to be happy without you

I hope that you've found happiness as well and you can find people and things that bring joy to you.

Day 25:

I suggested that we be friends again on day 22
I told you that I missed our conversation when in reality I just miss you
You're always okay with what I suggest so you accepted what I said
You responded "I would love that" When I suggested strictly friends
In a way I feel happy to have you back but deep down it still doesn't feel right
Because I am back in a place where I have you here but not in the way that I'd like
I don't want to be selfish, I don't want to be pushy, I don't want to do anything to hurt you
The only thing I want is to be together... All I want is you...
I am learning how not to have expectations
And how to love you without becoming attached
I hope that if I never have you the way I want, I can learn to be okay with that
I don't want to proceed with false intentions because deep down I still want more from you
I completely understand that you cannot give it I appreciate you telling me the truth

I received a call on day 24; it came from you and caught me by surprise

I miss how we could talk day in and day out without me somehow feeling deprived

I want to go back to the time before Mexico, when I assumed that you and I were together

When I made up my mind that what we had was perfect and it was sure to last forever

Because ever since I asked that dreadful question... the 'What are we" it has never since been the same

Because I poured out my heart, I told you I was falling and then you said that you couldn't catch me.

And since then I have continued falling with no safe place to land

I thought that I had it under control but now I'm in love with you and we're only friends

I tried to push you away so many times but it hurt me more to do so

and every time we come back together I gain another sense of false hope

Because chances are you'll never be mine and you will never fall in love with me

Love is not something that is forced I know it happens naturally

But you show up for me, you make me smile, you do everything correct to the tea
I just don't understand how it is that God didn't design you for me.

*It's easy for us to desire the kind of love that we
believe lives inside of someone else.*

You Pushed Me

Losing Balance

I don't have any empty spaces when I am with you.
It's like you fill every void and I become one with you.
I tell myself not to second guess all these feelings I am developing for you.
I tell myself that you are the real deal and I can put all my trust in you.
You prove my feelings right each and every time and my phone rings when I am thinking of you
It's like you can read my mind.
It's like you know me inside out I never have to tell you what I need.
It's like you know my heart and mind, it's like you just know me.
I feel like I can be myself and I try to be my best when I am with you.
I am a handful in every single way and it seems that's okay with you.
You never shut me down when I begin to talk too much and you stare deeply in my eyes to show me that you are someone I can trust.
You hold me close in the middle of the night & sometimes kiss my forehead.

You always ensure that I am comfortable; you always show me honor and respect.

I feel at ease when I am with you, you give me what I want and need.

I feel like you are a part of me and that God made you just for me.

Slipping

Since you come into my life, I have been making things right.

I have discovered parts of myself that you revealed with your light.

I have laughed more than I ever have; I have opened doors that were closed before I met you.

You have forced me to confront the old things in my life and introduced me to some new.

You made it possible for me to open up and you made a few of my prayers come true.

You made me feel special on so many occasions
That's how I began falling for you.

You listened to me talk so many times; always engaged and giving a listening ear.

You always showed me you had my back, you always eased my fears.

You were patient when I was upset; you did your best to make sure I knew that you cared.

You even showed up to my events even though at times I knew you didn't want to be there.

You motivated me to work on myself and on the problems deeply rooted in me.

You brought out a fire that has pushed me even further; you unlocked so many parts of me.

Falling

I looked above your head and I saw a shooting star...
I looked you in the eyes and then I heard your heart.
Something said that this was safe & I had nothing to worry about...
And as we walked you held my hand and it took away my very last doubt.
When we sat up high on the mountain top and looked over all the city
I found more beauty than the mountains themselves right in the moment you kissed me.
We spoke for hours about things we knew and we shared our intimate minds
and we enjoyed every second of every minute because we almost lost track of time.
We laughed at ourselves and the people around us the night you took me bowling on my birthday...
I laughed so hard at nearly everything you said I don't remember ever even keeping a straight face.
You beat me at every game that night & you told me you wouldn't just let me win
but I didn't care about winning any game... I just enjoyed the company I was in...

I watched you as you sat and studied out loud the night I came over your place to do my laundry...
& you never knew that I was staring at you but I'm glad you didn't catch me...
How amazing and driven and beautiful he is, were the thoughts that ran through my brain
and I only used my laundry as an excuse just so I could see you again.
On Valentine's Day, we were in the midst of disagreement and I expected nothing at all from you.
You showed up at my job with red roses in hand and a huge teddy bear balloon.
And when I called and cried because I was so frustrated you patiently listened and you calmed me down.
You knew just how to talk to me to make me come around.
The first time we spoke on the phone the night we met...
I didn't expect to even become so attached
We spoke like we'd known each other for years I guess meeting your soul mate can happen like that.

Hanging on for Dear Life

I remember when I started to fall for you,
That is where my deepest fears began.
I knew that it was then that it would trouble me if I ever lost you;
Those who have loved and lost would understand what that meant.
More and more you began expose all my pieces,
The ones I was aware of and ones I discovered only through you.
It puzzled me in many different ways how you had the ability to pull out my deepest truth.
It's like you eyeballed my soul, took it, and stored it right in your own soul and mind
Because no matter what I was thinking or feeling, you knew about it every time.
So I pushed you away as far as I could so you could have no more access to the depths of all that
I am
Because I knew that once you found that place, I would no longer stand a chance.
I would become this vulnerable little girl at mercy of your decision to love me or leave

and I just couldn't take the outcome of you walking away from me
If you left you would take me with you because already, I had given you my all.
It wasn't on purpose I tried to hold back but everything you were caused me to fall.
Emerged with my mind, emerged with my heart, intertwined with my body and soul
I became one with you and how I did it, I don't know.

Preparing For Landing

You are phenomenal but I just don't love you
You are the most amazing person I've ever met but I
just don't need you
You're so beautiful inside and out but I can't keep you
You're everything I want but I'm not ready for you
You make me really happy but I can live without you
You give me what I need but I just don't want you
You are the greatest in every way but just not enough
for me because I love someone else right now and
I'm not ready to set her free.

Shattering All Over the Ground

I painted a picture, one that only I could see;
A picture that said this was real and it would forever be you & me.
I told myself a lie, that you could never do any wrong;
That I could trust everything you told me because your respect for me was so strong.
I set myself up to only see the best shades of you.
I wiped out the signs and all of your past just to put you on a pedestal.
I couldn't see who you were because I wanted you to already be who you were becoming;
I thought you were already changed & that you knew the direction you were going.
Suddenly it fell apart when you finally showed me the truth.
The mask fell off and shattered on the ground and for the first time I saw the real you.
I was wrong for painting an image that said you were perfect and would never hurt me.
Your actions were the perfect inspiration to bring out the artist in me.

So I stand in my wrongs for giving you so much
credit and believing that you were the one
And now that I know that you are not,
I must gain the strength to move on.

Trying to Numb the Pain

Sleeping Soundly

I bought the dream you sold,
I allowed myself to just be; I gave you all my trust &
let you sweep me off my feet.
I melted in your arms and trusted that it was a safe
place to be
I let go, finally relaxed and fell into a deep sleep.
You then pinched me with reality but I just couldn't
wake up
You shook me and called my name but even that
wasn't enough
So there I stayed asleep while floating on a cloud
No way to snap out of my dream & no way to get
down
& the cloud began to disappear when you told me
that you didn't love me
I tried to learn how to fly but I did not have wings
When it finally evaporated, I began to fall at rapid
speeds
You were nowhere to be found, you were not there to
catch me
When I finally hit the pavement, I could not believe I
was still alive.

My heart was shattered, my mind was scattered, and I then wished I would have died.

There I laid in my own brokenness unable to move, unable feel.

I slowly began to go numb because the pain was too much to be real.

Woe' Man Down

There was a stray bullet with no name on it
That bullet happened to hit me
Dead in my heart I fell to the ground and I began to bleed
Gasping for air reaching for someone to come and hold me close
I know I am dying, I know that I'm fading; I just don't wanna be alone
But I see no one near, I hear nothing at all; all I feel is my senses getting weak
I try to say "somebody please help" but my lack of air won't let me speak
I feel the sensation in my heart, it's burning so deeply inside
I don't think I will live through this pain I don't think I will survive.

Morphine for the Heart

If I could choose, I would choose broken bones over a broken heart.
I would choose a crushed spleen over a crushed spirit.
I would choose being blind in my eyes over being blind in my mind.
I would choose to be abused physically rather than mentally or emotionally.
Because while trauma to my soul can take a toll on my entire existence,
Bones can be mended
Bruises can heal
but how can we overcome the emotional pain that we feel.
It's the kind of aching that sticks around sometimes for lifetimes
and no matter how hard we try
We can't press rewind;
to reverse the pain,
the trauma
and all of the emotional scars
So we walk through life with broken spirits
Cloudy minds

and shattered hearts.

I would rather feel the pain from a cut in my arm or even the consequence of a hangover from getting too drunk.

I want to numb the aching from my heart that is breaking.

I would rather hurt in my body because the pain is temporary;

Temporary but long enough to distract me from my dying soul

& long enough to kill the thoughts that often take control.

There's this pain, this terrible pain that only leaves when I am asleep

but sleep doesn't always go well because the trauma attacks me in my dreams.

I would choose to be choked until the room goes black and I am dizzy,

than to experience this depression that makes my life so weary.

I just want to feel good, someone please lead me to the cure

because I would do anything to feel this pain no more.

Take my health and take my limbs and replace it with joy and peace.
I would rather smile again,
laugh again
& get one full night of sleep.
Hear me out as I bargain,
The mental pain is too much to bear.
I will climb the highest mountain and swim the deepest sea if I could just find some comfort there.

Home Invasion

Stranger in my House

I wonder if you've ever felt the pain of which you have inflicted
I wonder if you've felt the emptiness that comes from losing everything internal and wishing that for just one second external things could fill in the missing pieces that were once filled with so much of my identity.
The pain is so much to bear,
So much to keep to the point where I can't eat
and to the point where I can't sleep.
Its' as if you grabbed my soul,
attached it to the bottom of your shoe
and decided to go on a marathon to promote my broken heart.
Who created you that way?
Who taught you that it was okay to come into the home of any person and ruin everything they've worked so tirelessly to build.
Your fingers, like termites;
Your eyes like mold;
Your words like guns going off in the night;
stealing every ounce of peace that used to fill this home.

The Shelter of my heart

You swung my heart wide open as if it was a mansion door and you walked in. You looked around and proceeded to make yourself comfortable. It was as if this was a place you could stay forever. You took off your shoes & then undressed yourself like you had known this place for years and never did I question rather or not my heart was a safe place for you to make a home. But I allowed you to stay. I allowed you to find peace with me, knowing that inside of you there was chaos. I believed that you had come in to rest so I let you rest in me and I fed you with the deepest parts of my soul. I wanted for you to understand that with me you would always be safe. But not I with you because when you entered into my space, you brought with you the pain & burdens of your past & you laid them on the shelf of my spirit. You brought with you confusion; you said it wouldn't be an issue & that you had everything under control so I trusted you to live in the home of my heart. But you didn't stay... When you felt better you decided that my heart was no longer a place fit for you & so you picked up & left but the confusion stayed, keeping company with pain. I then had to find a way to clean up the mess that you left behind. You used my heart as a hotel when it was always meant to be a home.

Not everyone deserves the key to your home
&
Nobody deserves the code to your safe.

Trying to Have a Heart for Revenge

But it won't heal me

I want to pay you back so bad and hurt you just like you hurt me.

I want to get revenge in the coldest kind of way but I know that won't set my heart free.

I want to tell her the truth and make you feel just like I do.

I want her to know your true colors and to see you just like I finally do.

I want to tell her that you'll cheat & that your apologies will never be sincere or true.

I want to tell her that while you were trying to win her back you were making me fall for you.

I want to tell her to refuse to trust you because you didn't truly wait for her return.

I want to tell her that what you tell her is lies and the lesson she tried to teach, you did not learn.

I want to send her all of the pictures. The ones we took with you adoring me.

I want to show her how you made me fall in love with you while still loving her secretly.

Bittersweet

I could be outright selfish and that is why my heart keeps longing for you. Maybe, I just can't stand the fact that you do her the way you did me. The way you made my heart throb, my back arch and my toes curl like Moraea Tortilis. I hate to imagine her being consumed by the grip of your palms; the palms that used to hold me. I may be having trouble being happy for you because I can't imagine someone stimulating your mind and spirit like I do. I don't know, I could be wrong on more levels than one but my view is distorted because of my desire for you. "Be happy for him" says my heart. "Let him be" says my mind but my ego screams the loudest crying out, "Show him who you are & everything he is missing."But who am I to determine that you are missing anything at all based on the absence of my presence?

I know I want the best for you, Even if that means I'm not the best for you but I don't want you to give your best to anyone but me. I hate to know that you will make her laugh with all of your best jokes, or make her cum with all of your best strokes or her body will be caressed by you and she will receive the care that you once gave to me. It's like you robbed me of yourself and gave it to someone else and I wonder if there is a possibility that I can come to genuinely cheer for you even if that means I lose.

Beginning to Heal

Moving Forward

I'm not looking forward to the process that involves forgetting about you
I'm not looking forward to the fact that my life will no longer include you
I'm not looking forward to the days where I wonder how you're doing
I'm not looking forward to the meeting new people or getting back into dating
I'm not looking forward to the fact that together we won't share anymore laughs
I'm not looking forward to finding another person to engage me in the kind of conversations we had
I'm not looking forward to starting all over and finding someone as amazing as you
but nonetheless I am moving on and beginning something new
I look forward to us both living in happiness
I look forward to us both finding success
I look forward to us both falling in love again
I look forward to us both receiving the best
I look forward to us being prosperous in everything we think and do

I look forward to us both rooting for each other, you're happy for me & I'm happy for you.

It's working for me

Take a deep breath and then exhale do it until you feel like you're okay.

Walk a great distance maybe a few miles do if you have to everyday.

Get plenty of sleep, rest your body and don't take on anything too great.

Experience silence so you can hear from me, don't allow chaos to consume your days.

Pray for yourself, do it out loud & speak what it is that you're looking for.

Open up your hands and open up your heart, make yourself available to receive more.

Look around at the world so big & take all of the beauty in.

And recognize the one who created everything is living deep within.

Learning to Love Myself Instead

The day I met you

I must've saw a "you" a million times before I got to know who you were.

I walked past you & we brushed shoulders and all we ever managed to say was, "excuse me."

I can't say I understand why we never took the time to be friendly with one another or even so much as exchange names;

Maybe we just weren't interested at the time.

I would stare at you and you would stare at me but it was like the only thing we had in common was our skepticism for one another.

Then came a day when I was alone and broken into pieces that I thought were beyond repair.

I picked myself up along with all my broken pieces and I began to walk.

As I moved along I was stopped dead in my tracks when I looked to my right and saw you standing there.

I locked eyes with you and I then noticed that you looked just as broken as I was;

But your spirit echoed as clear as my own thoughts and it whispered...

" I understand."

It was as if you unlocked my soul & had already fallen in once I'd stood up tall and & told you my name.

In that very moment, there was no division between the two of us.

As we spoke I learned things about you so I told you how beautiful you were.

I told you that you were intelligent, strong, amazing and finally I worked up the confidence to utter 3 more words.

These words fell from my lips as if my lips were the cliffs that make way for the rivers of Niagara.

These words came forth, out of the depths of my belly, gently kissed the universe and formed

"I love you."

How the tears began to fall from my eyes because this surge of joy then struck me by surprise

Because, finally, I had met the one person who had the ability to set my soul on fire.

I looked you in your eyes once more; this time certain of the truth I was preparing to speak & boldly, I said again

"I love you."

You smiled...

With a confidence that showed your belief in the words that I had just spoken.

I then understood that it was always you that I needed.

I needed to understand who you were as much as I needed you to understand me.

That day I discovered the depths and vast seas of a person that I had seen but ignored for my entire life.

That was the first time in my life that I was able to see someone so clear.

I finally reached out my hand to touch you.

You imitated me & you did the same.

Palm to palm our hands came together beginning at both of our fingertips.

Your hand was cold; like glass windows on a winter night in Baltimore.

But I appreciated your chilling hand, for I had not come to you for warmth.

I only reached to make certain that you were actually there and my greatest breakthrough came when I accepted that I had introduced myself to the girl in the mirror.

Now What Do You See?

I love the way I fit my clothes

I love the way I wear my hair

I love the shade of skin I'm in

I love to see my face without makeup

Just natural and bare

I love to stand in the mirror and thank God for whom

he made me to be

I love that I am no longer imprisoned by what the

world thinks of me

I love the tone in my arms
I love the thickness of my thighs
I love the plumpness of my lips
I love the creases in my eyes
I love the arch in my back
I love the stretch marks on my legs
I love the height that I stand at

I love my big forehead

I love the muscles I see when I flex the muscles in

my abdomen

I love that I can see beauty in the curves of my

midsection

I am fearfully and wonderfully made, I am happy

with how I appear. I never needed to change my

being I just had to change my perception of the girl in

the mirror.

I am Her; She is Me

I am a river of flowing waters
The Flower that grows without force,
The root inside every tree
The Soiled land beneath your toes
The breeze that kisses your forehead
The rising sun at the crack of dawn
The hot cocoa you sip when it's cold outside
The taste buds at the tip of your tongue
I am the sound of a roaring sea
The wings of a soaring bird
The nectar inside of a ripened peach
The sentence that brings life to every word
I am love I am light
I am the salt of the Earth
I am a city set on top of a hill
I can finally see my worth
I am worth far more than rubies
Even the hairs on my head are numbered
I am a royal priesthood
There is a King of all Kings &
I am His daughter

Take a big bite of who you are and chew until you taste every ingredient of your existence. Once you do, go out into the world and feed the multitude with soul food that is hidden in the depths of your belly.

This is Forgiveness

For me not for you

I just want to tell you I forgive you for all the pain you brought to my life
I just want to tell you I forgive you for making me believe every lie
I just want to tell you I forgive you for making a fool of me
I just want to tell you I forgive you for making me think there was something wrong with me
I just want to tell you I forgive you for stealing my light to escape the darkness in your life
I just want to tell you I forgive you for not being able to live up to all the hype
I just want to tell you I forgive you for making a mess and then leaving me to clean it up
I just want to tell you I forgive you for making me believe you were someone I could trust
I'm no longer angry with you; I'm no longer in pain.
I'm no longer a broken hearted individual & from this situation I had so much to gain
So now I just want to say thank you for the amazing role that you played
Because so much new life grew inside of me from the times that you brought me rain.

Thank you!

Thank you for helping me break bondages

Thank you for setting me free

Thank you for forcing me to love myself even after learning that you didn't love me

Thank you for letting me walk away

Thank you for not chasing behind

Thank you for letting me heal my spirit, my heart and even my mind

Thank you for seeing how imperfect I was

Thank you for making me feel like I wasn't enough

Thank you for bringing out the passion for me to fill those empty spaces with intense self love

Thank you for choosing her

Thank you for letting me go

Thank you for leaving me in the dirt,

It became the soil that helped me grow

Thank you for finishing me off

Thank you for putting me out of my misery

Thank you for being my breaking point from all the patterns in my history

Thank you for being the reason that I finally put myself first

Thank you for making me better by bringing me to my worst.

All pain is temporary but we make it permanent when we refuse to deal with the root of what caused it. Feel the pain Deal with the source of the pain and heal it. There are no shortcuts.

Accepting Validation from God

My Temple

I came to understand something after carefully examining my past. I came to understand that every time I gave my body away, I gave away my power. I handed over my greatest possession. It is not the pleasing aspect of my body that makes it my most powerful possession but it is what my body is capable of. My body is the holder of life; it is a sustainer of humanity through God himself. My body is the home of soul and the vessel I use for EVERYTHING I do. My body is my existence. My body is my church of which God must dwell. Whenever I abuse and misuse my body, I give away my entire identity in exchange for a temporary pleasure; pleasure that only lasts but a few moments. Why do we give our power away to complete strangers? People whom, once receiving that power, totally reject its beauty. I understand now why God wants our bodies to be undefiled. Why He asks us to preserve it and walk in purity. Every time I gave my body away there was a knowing, a conviction that I had sold myself short and traded my crown for an orgasm. My eyes were opened to the fact that I felt ashamed and dirt low after sex because I exchanged something of such high value for something that was temporary. Our bodies are our everything and that is why God gave each of us just one. We cannot swap it out when it goes bad and we cannot live without it. When we give it away or abuse it, we wrong ourselves entirely and decrease the divinity of it. We must preserve and protect our bodies.

Be Still and Know

My fears are not real.

My Anxieties are not real.

Every time I allow myself to feel afraid or anxious I make the decision to live in a lie.

God has not given me the spirit of fear but of power and of love and of a sound mind.

God has not called me to be anxious.

All things are working for my good.

God has heard my prayers and he wants to give me the desires of my heart.

In order for me to receive, I must believe that it is already finished.

God has never broken one of his promises or failed at keeping his word.

I can trust Him with my love life.

I can trust Him with my finances.

I can trust Him with my health.

I can trust Him with my entire life.

God is trustworthy.

I will not pity myself for the things I don't yet have but I will bless the Lord for all I do have while I wait for all the things I have prayed for.

Things to Remember

God will send many people to teach you;
Make sure you learn from them.
Everyone that comes into your life is not for keeping.
Love people without becoming attached, for then, if they do leave at the appointed time, you will not be hurt but instead wiser.
Shine your light in the lives of others but do not give your light away.
People must find their own light otherwise they will take yours and leave you in utter darkness.
Every broken person is not your assignment.
Your job is not to save anyone; your job is to point them to the savior.
In the process guard your heart, guard your mind, protect your peace & never punish yourself for loving someone who could not love you in return.

On Repeat

I am not afraid to love and be loved.

I am not what happened to me.

I am surrounded by people who genuinely love me and support me.

I am not seeking validation from romantic relationships.

I am not seeking the familiar feelings of rejection, unworthiness or inadequacy.

I am no longer looking for love but instead, love is looking for me.

I accept others and others accept me.

I am worthy to be loved, cherished and valued.

I am attracting people who add light to my life.

I am walking in wholeness.

I am not lacking in any area of my life.

I am not my past and my past is not me.

I am not what my parents did or didn't do.

I am not a carrier of heartbreak.

I am at peace and I spread peace wherever I go.

*Every time you overcome something new,
you prove that there is NOTHING
you can't get through.*

Gather the Pieces

Kylelashay is a first time author, motivational speaker, spoken word artist and youth mentor. She is mostly known for her Social media videos and has gone viral more than 3 times. Kylelashay developed a passion for writing early on in life, beginning to write short stories at age eight & going on to write poetry around age nine or ten. Currently her focus is primarily on controversial and cultural issues. Kylelashay's primary mission in life is to reach this generation and to ignite new fires in the hearts of each person she encounters.

To learn more about the author visit:
www.Kylelashaydraper.com
Or email: Kylelashaydraper@gmail.com

Made in United States
Cleveland, OH
11 January 2025

13265710R00083